Bulimia to Balance

Aeryon Ashlie

Bulimia to Balance Copyright © 2018 by Aeryon Ashlie.

All rights reserved. No part of this book may be used or reproduced in any manner whatsoever without written permission except in the case of brief quotations embodied in critical articles or reviews.

Disclaimer: Although the author and publisher of this book have made every effort to ensure that the information in this book was correct at press time, the author and publisher do not assume and hereby disclaim any liability to any party for any loss, damage, or disruption caused by errors or omissions, whether such errors or omissions result from negligence, accident, or any other cause.

Always check with your doctor before undertaking any new health regimen.

For more information of programs, speaking engagements and events Aeryon Ashlie can be reached at www.aeryonashlie.com

ISBN: 978-1-7751232-3-1

Cover photo by Ingrid Paul Photography.

Published by Aeryon Ashlie.

First Edition: January 2018

Table of Contents

Introduction v
Chapter 1: Eating Disorders 1
Chapter 2: The Battle 8
Chapter 3: The Effects 15
Chapter 4: The Fitness Game 17
Chapter 5: The Rebound 20
Chapter 6: The Turning Point 22
Chapter 7: Sick and Tired 23
Chapter 8: Reflection 26
Chapter 9: My Why 30
Chapter 10: Planned Meals 32
Chapter 11: Trigger Foods 36
Chapter 12: No Scale 38
Chapter 13: Journaling 40
Chapter 14: Support 43
Chapter 15: Anxiety 45
Chapter 16: Affirmations 47
Chapter 17: Tapping 51
Chapter 18: Breathing 53
Chapter 19: Exercise 55

Chapter 20: Supplements.................................57
Chapter 21: Mindfulness................................59
Chapter 22: Goal Setting...............................63
Chapter 23: Forgiveness................................66
Chapter 24: CBT Therapy................................68
Chapter 25: Nasty Girl.................................70
Chapter 26: Bulimia My Friend..........................73
Chapter 27: Creating a New Story.......................75
Chapter 28: Bulimia to Balance.........................77
About the Author, Aeryon Ashlie 79

Introduction

In sharing my journey with you, I want to be clear: I am not offering any 'Magic Pills' or easy solutions that will fix all of your food or health related issues. Instead, what I can share with you is my own personal experience with dieting and eating disorders, as well as the tools I have used to manage how I am eating with what is going on in my life. My experience may resonate with you as I have learned to accept who I am and then gather support around me. My intention is that this book will start a conversation regarding the power of our internal dialogue, fitness, health and nutrition. No matter what you are struggling with, until you shift your perception and create positive reinforcement, your negative mindset will win.

The goal of this book is to learn to confront the 'negative voices' that we face, and for each person to find the tools and strategies for fitness and health sustainability. I have learned the power that results in sharing our stories. When others shared their experiences with me around eating disorders, I felt 'normalized' in my own experience. I didn't need to be ashamed. I was not alone. I hope my story will encourage others seeking journey to a healthy loving relationship with self and others.

Before I begin, I want to emphasize that if you are having issues with an eating disorder, I hope that you can reach out to your local Eating Disorder (ED) clinic. They offer resources that can provide support, counselling and guidance.

Chapter 1
Eating Disorders

My name is Aeryon Ashlie. I am a Mother, Holistic Nutritional Coach, Eating Disorder Recovery Coach, On Air Radio Personality, Certified Trainer and have been a part of the Canadian Health and Fitness Industry for over 14 years. For 22 years I was struggling with a negative body image, binge eating, chronic dieting and bulimia. When looking at my credentials and background, most people would think I should have this figured out. I have the tools, yet I still was held hostage for countless years by my mental struggle. How could I have an eating disorder? More importantly, how could no one have known….

There are three commonly recognized eating disorders, which are not necessarily independent of one another.

First, Anorexia. Anorexia is the most physically recognizable food-related mental health issue, which results when an individual restricts food due to an unbalanced body weight perception.

Second, is the eating disorder I experienced, Bulimia, which the **Merriam-Webster** dictionary notes is characterized by compulsive overeating, followed by self-induced vomiting or the use of a laxative or diuretic abuse. This eating disorder can easily go undetected, as someone with bulimia can have a "normal" weight, or be overweight.

The third eating disorder is a newly categorized disorder called Binge eating disorder. Binge eating disorder happens in two steps;

first, the person eats copious amounts of food, and then, they might take laxatives, exercise profusely, or possibly restrict calories the following day. The result of binge eating disorder, as with all eating disorders, is an unbalanced and unhealthy diet regime. Often these intertwine, occurring at the same time, or they can be independent disorders.

However, Bulimia and Binge Eating are similar because they result in extreme shame and guilt after an episode. In the beginning, these often start as a weight solution but as time progresses it turns into a mental game of control and numbing.

According to ANAD (National Association of Anorexia Nervosa and Associated Disorders), over thirty million people in North America suffer from some kind of an eating disorder or disordered eating.

Those with eating disorders have a significant elevated mortality rate, due to the complications and complexity of the issues related to eating disorders, such as depression, poor nutrition, heart and organ health and anxiety.

The demographic tends to be women, and usually, those involved in athletics, especially competitive sports.

The typical age group was once thought to be between the ages of 18-25; however, based on recent studies and anecdotes/ experiences from the women I engage with, eating disorders do not have an age limit. The age demographic of eating disorders do not end at 25. Most who suffered in their youth still have food related issues except now they are Mothers, Fathers, professionals, etc. functioning in society. It is difficult to quiet the inner voice that has dominated so much of one's life. Those who have shared with me express how hard it is to consider requesting support to change negative eating lifestyles that have plagued them for years.

All Women's Talk (.com) outlines the seven Eating Disorder Personality traits that contribute to the start or continuation of an ED:

1. Perfectionism
2. OCD
3. Constant Need for More
4. All or Nothing
5. Low Self Esteem
6. Very Emotional
7. Fearful.

What stands out for me from this list is that eating disorders surface not simply from a desire to 'look' a certain way, but also as the result of a range of mental health and stress factors. I know that I can personally identify with some, if not all of these traits to some degree. The need to feel in control in all I do, especially in stressful times, brings me some sense of safety and security. When tail spinning in a binge, the release of letting myself go in overeating created an almost euphoric feeling of release. There was no need to be 'in control.' It felt calming to just eat and eat. However, after the binge I was angry with myself, feeling out of control, and then I would purge to gain back the feeling of control. It did not occur to me that the feeling of control and dealing with my current feelings was what I needed to confront, facing emotional issues, and habits of binging.

According to ULi feline (.com) factors that can also play a part are the following:

Genetics. Studies show people with eating disorders tend to have someone in their family who also suffers from an ED. My Aunt suffered from a mixture of Bulimia and Anorexia and two of my cousins had issues with Anorexia and Bulimia. As a child, food and our bodies had always been an important topic at dinners and family gatherings. To this day, at family functions dessert is a no-no and everyone is always concerned with things being fat-free, gluten-free, low-sugar, etc.

Learning how to eat healthy from a young age is a wonderful lesson, however when the focus is heavily on how food affects your looks; it can definitely cause issues.

Biochemistry. Another important factor. People with an Eating Disorder tend to have a higher level of cortisol, which is a hormone released when we face stressful or uncontrollable situations.

> Cortisol is a steroid hormone, commonly known as the stress hormone,[1] is produced by the adrenal glands. It can take only minutes for you to feel the effects of cortisol in the face of stress. The release of this hormone takes a multi-step process involving two additional minor hormones.
>
> First, the part of the brain called the amygdala[2] has to recognize a threat. This then sends a message to the part of the brain called the hypothalamus,[3] which releases corticotrophin-releasing hormone (CRH). CRH signals the pituitary gland to release adrenocorticotropic hormone (ACTH), which signals the adrenal glands to produce cortisol.
>
> In survival mode, the *optimal* amounts of cortisol can be life saving. It helps to maintain fluid balance and blood pressure, and regulates certain body functions that aren't crucial in the moment, such as the reproductive drive, immunity, digestion and growth.
>
> However, when one is continuously stressed with an issue (i.e. food, body image, etc.) the body *constantly* releases cortisol, and chronic elevated levels can lead to serious issues.[4] Too much cortisol can suppress the immune system, increase blood pressure and sugar, decrease libido, produce acne, contribute to obesity and more.

---

[1] https://medlineplus.gov/ency/article/003693.htm
[2] http://www.huffingtonpost.ca/entry/body-stress-response_n_2902073
[3] http://www.huffingtonpost.ca/entry/body-stress-response_n_2902073
[4] http://www.huffingtonpost.ca/entry/stress-health-effects-cancer-immune-system_n_2599551

Becoming aware of how anxiety feels and how it hits in certain situations is key. Some commonly recognized calming tools such as meditation, mantras, and supplements can be very beneficial when recognizing high personal anxiety.

Supporting and relieving yourself from constant stress is very important. I am now very aware when my anxiety is kicking in and the importance of positive self talk in order to not allow my anxiety and actions to escalate. Choosing words of love, gratitude, empowerment, forgiveness are all key in centering myself.

Fear of losing control. When we have a fear of losing control in certain areas of our lives, it can manifest in our dieting, with the need to control and regulate our food and eating habits, while other areas of our lives feel uncontrollable. With the 'all or nothing' mentality, I would either be fully engaging in either dieting or binging. There was no healthy in-between, and because I seemed to operate at 'highs and lows,' I became addicted to the ups and downs. It often seemed like the only solution. This self-understanding was a real eye opener. Where I also made a connection was the similar pattern in other areas of my life, as I inhabited a space of extremes (relationships, finances, exercise, etc.). I have always been a strong woman who is self-reliant, viewing control as essential. Letting go of the need for control has been a healing process, and allowed me to live in moderation, not only in relation to food, but in areas such as relationships and financial matters. I have been learning to have structure as opposed to concrete control, with understanding how to incorporate flexibility. This has become essential in every area of my life.

Environment. Our environment plays another huge factor, which can include home and school life. Perhaps the individual was bullied or peer pressured at home or at school about their weight. These environmental factors develop into mental and habitual patterns that seem to follow us our whole lives. Growing up, there was always an emphasis on my weight and how I looked. In school I was bullied relentlessly which led to my belief that I was "not enough" and "too much. I believed that if I could just lose weight, I would be accepted and finally happy.

Culture: I'm sure it comes as no surprise to you that we live in a culture saturated with slogans that seem geared to make us feel inadequate. We are bombarded daily by television and magazine articles that tell us that we are not skinny enough, healthy enough or fit enough. Just look at the newsstand at your local grocery store; every cover is awash with pictures of bodies or 'easy' solutions to 'get that perfect figure!' Even though we can be aware of the external pressure, there is no denying that we are drawn to aesthetically pleasing items, be it a person, flowers, a car etc. So, in that, each of us have created this fake "perfect" physical list that we believe once we achieve will lead to true happiness. Although most of us agree that nothing exterior can bring true long-lasting happiness, it does not diminish the desire we may often feel for a certain image.

Numbing. As a society we abuse drugs, alcohol, gambling, shopping and social media as a means to tune out or numb. It is no surprise that food would fall into this category. Food addiction or food related issues are often a result of the need to not feel. By filling with food we essential stuff our emotions. I know that the greatest awareness for myself has been standing in my emotions and not eating them.

With these factors, personality traits and shame, it is no surprise that eating disorders are still prevalent. Living in a culture where we have so much, our daily problems are not just survival. We have the ability to spend time obsessing over looks and obtaining the perfect Abs, Butt, Skin, Car, Job, etc. This unrealistic pursuit continues to lead young men and women in the direction of chasing this "Perfect Ideal." Trying to feel fulfilled and satisfied with things such as money, food, body image or status and an inner dialogue focused on those thoughts, can leave us exhausted and unsatisfied with who we are, how we look and how we are feeling. At some point, we hopefully realize it is relationships, healthy living, loving ourselves (flaws and all), feeling our emotions and finding our own passions in life that brings the most contentment and joy. My eating disorder became the mirror that reflected back and made me realize what I really wanted in my life.

In my youth, I never realized the long-term damage I was causing to not just my mental relationship surrounding food but also my body. Depending on the severity and length of time the person has struggled with an ED, this will determine the effects both physically and mentally.

For example, with bulimia, the long-term effects can include gum disease, tooth decay, and/or poor eyesight from the pressure of purging. Other effects can be the increased likelihood of osteoporosis, heart issues, tears in the esophagus, fainting from low blood pressure, and kidney disease. Feelings of hopelessness and mental fatigue can unfortunately lead to suicide. In my early 20's I started experiencing random blackouts and had to wear a heart monitor for several days to confirm that I did not have an irregular heart beat. However, the doctors were unaware of my continuous private battle with bulimia.

Eating disorders can also have an extremely detrimental effect on one's quality of life.

One of the biggest issues I experienced was the effect on my relationships from the social withdrawal. I remember being with my partner and feeling panicked to be at his family home for the holidays because I could not escape to a bathroom if I was triggered by something I ate. I avoided all social gatherings and anything that required food and drink, as I knew it would eventually lead me to a binge and purge.

I was always dieting which was my way not only to have control but also my excuse to not have to eat anything except my rigid food program. My personal battle waged on from the age of 14-36.

Chapter 2

The Battle

This is my story.

My Mother was a high-level figure skating coach, and my father was a hobby bodybuilder. Needless to say, athletics and aesthetics were always very important growing up in our household. I remember as early as kindergarten being chased in the playground and called names. As I entered elementary I was labeled the "chunky" or "thick" girl. I quickly learned to define myself by these labels, I grew to hate school and my body. In grade three, due to the bullying, my parents finally decided that home-schooling me would be the best solution. The years I was home schooled we lived on a farm in the interior of BC and the pressure to look a certain way was not a part of my life except from my parents, who were concerned with my size and eating habits, and still watched my food intake.

At the age of 10 my grandmother's husband made sexual advances on me. I believe I never spoke of the sexual abuse until years later was because it had been in a swimming pool and the abuse was genital touching not penetration. The past several years, while digging deep and doing the work, I have looked at the connection between my ED, my constant need to feel validated, and this event. The secrecy, self-doubt, and then the issues I had with older men in my childhood all now connect. I never thought that this violation affected my life choices but in hindsight I now see how it definitely contributed.

In sexual abuse there is confusion of thinking you are to blame or in my case, we were just playing in the pool. This led to doubt my own internal guide. I never identified what he did as sexual assault until much later.

In grade six I returned to public school, and the teasing resumed. Looking back at photos I see a strong, healthy girl but my parents were adamant to help me get control over my eating. I know it pained them to see their daughter sad and ostracized from her peers. I remember my mother bringing me shakes at lunch in attempts to help me with my weight loss. However, I would go home after school and eat till I could not move, trying to numb my emotions. By the age of 13, my parents enrolled me in the Weight Watchers program with the hope of helping me gain some control and understanding over food. Sitting in those meetings with 30+-year age women, I quickly learned that I was too much and not enough, all at the same time. The weekly weigh-ins and extra attention to my already negative body image did not help at all. I began to view food as my enemy, which I would carry with me for many years to come.

After Weight Watchers I became obsessed with calories. It was then I found frozen weight control meals, which then became my only food. At a young age my goal and idea was that being skinny would bring me fulfillment. After all, everybody was so focused on my body. If I could control this then maybe I would be happy. Not only would my parents approve of me specifically my father, but also I could be in that elusive popular junior high school group that was always unreachable. Later, this void transferred to other areas of my life that I needed fulfilled.

I remember at this time I began to shrink away from my family. I would take all food to my room and eat. I was secluding myself. I had no relationship with my father, who struggled to communicate with me and my mother was trying to hold the family together.

I remember my father would get upset at my weight gain and over eating. In looking back it was the only time I received the much-desired attention from him. The more he monitored, the more I ate.

It was in those years that the social angst at school also added to the pressure. I wanted to be one of the pretty, thin popular girls but I was never "enough." I was always the "Big Boned" or "Bigger girl" or so I believed. To me the only reason why I could not reach this social status had to be my body.

At the age of 14, my friend was sharing his family's distress at watching his sister suffer from Bulimia and Anorexia. He explained how she was not eating and then when she did eat she would vomit and hide it under the bed. His sister was starting a treatment program and was extremely thin and unhealthy. All I heard in the conversation was *she got to eat and was thin*.

This idea was foreign to me. I had never heard of an eating disorder before. The fact that she was able to eat mass amounts of food, throw it up, and still lose weight appealed to that little girl who had struggled with body issues her whole life.

In hindsight I also see how this gave me a payout in several ways. My dad still gave me the attention I craved from over eating and I would finally be able to be accepted by the 'cool' kids.

So in my grade eight sense of rational this seemed like a winning solution. *"I could do that!!"* I thought to myself. Finally, I could finally win over a problem that everyone had always said I had.

I vividly remember being excited as I went home that very afternoon. I proceeded to stuff myself silly with food, and then retreated to the bathroom to purge. It was not easy at first but as I did it more and more it became easy.

Over the next year, I adopted my new weight loss habit every day, and at all occasions. I did not even see the harm I was causing or the consequences of my actions long-term. At first, I did lose weight. This new habit allowed me to enter the social world I had always felt excluded from, which is interesting, as years later this "diet tool" that opened doors for me became the ultimate closure. I finally began to get noticed, and for the first time, even had some boys take an interest in me.

However, as time progressed, my newfound diet consumed all aspects of my life. In my teens I played guitar and sang in local talent shows. I was chosen to be a singer/dancer in the Young Canadians of the Calgary Stampede. I recall many practices where I was barely able to sing. My throat was so raw from the constant vomiting that I sounded raspy and hitting notes was challenging. One factor that dominated much of my life was that any event that involved food became an extremely stressful situation (pizza day, parties). I would scan for a bathroom and preplan my purge. I would always start with the plan to not overindulge, however one extra chip or a treat would instantly turn me into Bulimic Aeryon.

Now the best way to describe Bulimic Aeryon is she is a different person. There is no rationale. Once she showed up, I became consumed with my binge. No one and nothing could get in my way. My anxiety at that point was so overwhelming and all I wanted to do was to consume as much as I could and then get rid of it.

In my teens I was friends with several girls who regularly binged and purged. It almost became a game. We would binge then purge at the same time, watching out for each other so others would not know.

At 16 my Father caught me in the act. I had thought my new "diet tool" had gone unnoticed until I was in a fight with my parents. Our relationship was very unhealthy and my dad shouted back at me that he heard me throwing up one day. I remember my mother's shocked face as she turned to me. "Is this true?" she asked, then proceeded to ask me why I would waste food. In hindsight she wishes she had never spoken to me that way. She says now that would have changed much of her parenting, and over time she returned to university and became a teacher and guidance counsellor. When she has young girls who come in with parent issues or ED issues she uses my story as an example to them. (And how parents can be so 'blind' to their children's issues needing to learn positive and caring communication).

As I stormed downstairs to my room I promised it would never happen again; I was let off the hook.

However, I just became more tactical, moving a radio into the washroom, playing it with the turned on the shower and sink taps. I became an expert at flushing the toilet exactly at the right time of a purge. So my promise of stopping never even started.

At 16, after being kicked out of 3 schools for lack of attendance, I quit school entirely. My father's stance on not participating in my education was that I would start working to pay for rent etc. I worked at the Movie Theatre, KFC and go-go danced at night with fake id on the weekend.

In the 1980's and early 1990's employees at KFC and Famous Players were allowed to bring home the leftovers. I would bring home these gigantic bags of popcorn and buckets of chicken, sneaking them into my bedroom where I would binge till I could barely move. I learned very quickly what was an easy purge, and if you speak with most Bulimics they all have their go-to foods. Mine was and remained popcorn for many years, which stems from this early experience. This is followed by cake batter later on – which can easily become a trigger food for me even to this day. As I proceeded through my later teens the episodes were constant.

Go-go dancing on Friday and Saturday nights in a local nightclub was something I loved. This was the first time I had people watch me and I loved being admired. I looked and acted much older and using a relative's ID was not a stretch. Plus, I was paid, which bought more food.

As the years progressed I now see the pattern of always being on the hunt to fill and numb, be it food, boys, money, shopping. I was searching for something to give me a feeling of being enough and to numb out any unwanted emotions that arose. I always had a boyfriend, and in hindsight my need for male attention and approval was a constant issue.

At the age of 18 my parents got divorced, and my dad finally told me for the first time he loved me. I remember we had gone for dinner for my birthday and he gave me a card (which I still have) and I sat in my car in the parking lot and I sobbed uncontrollably.

It was in this time I began to hang out with the "wrong" crowd. I was partying, on the streets, involved in drugs and drinking. Looking back at this time in my life, I see now that it was risky but I saw no consequence. The truth is I did not care. I did not even think of the future.

It was just *get through the day. Get to the next binge.*

I was falling into a hard and short lifestyle. At twenty-one, by the grace of God or the Universe working her magic, I was given the opportunity to move to Toronto. However, I then lived alone with no one to monitor me. My eating disorder was in full swing and I added in 2-3 times a day for gym sessions. I was running, training hard, but fully binging and purging with almost every meal. I was never happy physically and I was still never enough. The downside was now I was not losing the weight. In fact, I was gaining.

Shorty after my move to Toronto, my brothers joined me and together we started a Pet Supply Company. With the store this enabled multiple bathrooms at both business and home. I remember many nights where I would get triggered. Leaving home I would visit multiple fast-food drive-ins, grocery stores, binging on as much food as possible, and then heading to our Pet Store and purging. With a bathroom off site, my secret was contained. I remember many occasions where I sat crumbled on the floor in front of the toilet, sobbing uncontrollably after a binge. I felt lost, hopeless and overwhelmed by my illness.

My life came to revolve around this binge and purge cycle. And once again, I became socially ostracized because I was afraid of going out. My clothes did not fit. I felt uncomfortable in my skin. The idea of being triggered, and not finding a place to purge created such a high level of anxiety that I avoided all situations.

Throughout the years I carefully strategized the family get-togethers and I knew where the bathrooms were and how to time my "showers" around a binge and purge. I cannot remember any holiday that I did not purge, especially if there was alcohol. Oddly enough I never tried to avoid alcohol, as it became my justification for my lack of willpower. The need to control my surroundings haunted me, isolated me, and I was starting to have serious health consequences.

Chapter 3
The Effects

These health issues continue to affect me to this day. For example, as the enamel on my teeth started to wear and my trips to the dentist were becoming a regular activity. Starting in my early twenties, I had my first 2 teeth pulled. At the time were so infected, the freezing would not take. I remember sobbing the whole time, the pain was so intense. The molars had disintegrated so badly that the dentist had to pull them out piece by piece. However, that physical pain was still not enough to cause me to stop.

Over the past 20 years, I have had to pay well over $50,000 on dental work. All of my top teeth are veneers and implants. I have had numerous extractions, and every one of my teeth has had a filling. It was a common occurrence for my teeth to crumble and break apart.

My eyesight began to worsen due to the physical pressure that comes from constant purging. Someone from a blog post once described this pain as, "Like a weird pain, almost like there isn't room for my eyes," which I think captures this experience quite accurately. The constant pressure from purging was enormous. I had such bad eyesight that when I finally got my laser eye surgery, I could barely see anything right in front of me.

My knuckles developed sores from my teeth rubbing on them against my molars as I repeatedly shoved my fingers down my throat. I became so skilled that at times; I could just flex my stomach muscles in order to create the purge. On many occasions, I lost my voice, and I would use lozenges because my throat was constantly raw. My face would swell from the pressure, my eyes looked bloodshot, and often the sodium of the binge would cause immense water retention so the next day I felt worse which then led to another binge.

Acne also plagued my chin and sores from the corners of my mouth as I would have to often jam my fingers down my throat to activate my stomach reflexes.

By far, though, the worst part was the mental trauma that resulted from all of this. The anxiety that surrounded food was intense; every time I ate, I was confronted with this lack of control that had come to affect every part of who I was. In addition to this was the horrible guilt and shame that followed my episodes, which worsened over time. Every time I purged, I told myself, *"This is the last time."* Inevitably, one extra bite of food would trigger me, and I would spiral into the same patterns of body shame and purging. Vivid nightmares of consuming mass amounts of food and not finding a location to purge, would lead to waking up in a state of panic.

For many years my diet trick no longer worked. Each week and day, I would swear I would stop and eat properly. Only I did not even know what that was. My ability to consume so much food at one time created a constant hunger.

In a binge and purge, you never get rid of all the calories you consume. Your body will naturally absorb some of them. Time would then become a huge factor whenever I would binge. My anxiety would spike overwhelmingly in these moments, as every second that the food was in my body, was another second I thought I was gaining weight. I would shove food down my throat and then almost sprint to the bathroom looking for release.

Chapter 4
The Fitness Game

In my late 20's I sold the Pet Store and moved to New York for a number of years with my wealthy older boyfriend. He promised me a career in singing and that he would bring me to the level in my career I always wanted.

However, I was his arm candy, to say the least.

This enabled the lifestyle I always wanted, including fancy cars, trips, and money but I was still struggling with my bulimia and the promise of my career in singing was not becoming a reality.

Eating one evening at a fine restaurant on Soho, I remember retracting to the bathroom to throw up a beautiful carb rich meal we had enjoyed. The several years with him were riddled with highly verbally abusive behaviour, especially when he drank. He always held his money and influence over my head. He repeatedly told me I was nothing without him and the control of money and power he had over me was overwhelming. In hindsight the only thing that I could control was what stayed in my stomach.

It was the spring of 2001 that I finally made the decision to leave. He was away for business and while he was gone I packed my things into my truck and headed back to Toronto. My aunt, who lived in New York, helped me orchestrate everything, as I was concerned about his brothers who lived in the same building and had keys to the condo. It was a middle-of-the-night-flee as I left a note and drove back home.

Once back in Canada, I started working as a personal trainer at a Fitness Gym in Toronto. Although I was still not in control of my own food issues, I did love helping others reach their fitness goals.

Plus no one knew my secret.

Working at a gym allowed me the time to train my clients and have extra opportunity for my own workouts. This additional training furthered my weight loss goals. Plus, many of the driven, focused, and wonderful people working in the fitness industry surrounded me daily.

In the spring of 2002, I was encouraged by some of my friends and colleagues to compete in an upcoming fitness competition. For my first competition, I chose to compete in my home province of Alberta since my mother lived in Calgary, this location was perfect for a visit and home base while competing. The girl who helped me through my first show basically moved in with me for the last 3 weeks. She monitored everything I ate and helped me through the process. I was a little apprehensive at first, but I decided it might be fun to try at least once. I'm so glad that I made that choice.

One of the most surprising factors that resulted from training for my fitness competitions was the positive effect it had on my eating disorder. After years of never having control over food, the structure of the competition enabled me to stay focused on my end goal. I was adhering to a set diet and meal plan. I had tried and failed at diets for many years before, but this time, I had a powerful "Why."

I wanted to be successful in the fitness show. This desire to succeed and feel accepted, felt very similar to what I experienced as a child and teen. The result of this focus had the effect of taming my urges to binge. I had told everyone I was doing a show and I could not let them down or myself. Plus it was the first time I stuck to a plan.

I became disciplined.

There were no more triggers. I did not buy certain foods that previously triggered my eating binges. I was focused and had something to explain my new eating habits. I also changed the thoughts that were running through my mind, with positive post it notes, reading books that were uplifting, and choosing conversations with others who were supportive and caring. I was in a positive mindset with my goals and I became happier, as I was not in a constant state of guilt.

There was no more bulimia.

For the first time in my life, I felt free from the illness that had always haunted me.

I finally felt truly in control.

After 14 weeks of strict dieting I flew to Calgary and I placed 3rd which then qualified me for the Nationals in Toronto. After a weekend of some treats, which I felt extremely guilty for enjoying I jumped back into intense training and dieting for Nationals.

As the next show date came closer I remember looking in the mirror astounded at the transformation my body had made. I looked like I always wanted to look. I had muscle definition. I looked lean. I felt fantastic and, in my mind, I was cured!!! I thought if I could just continue following this lifestyle then surely I would never have this issue again.

At this time I reached out to a fitness magazine, Oxygen that had been a constant source of inspiration over the years. I was excited to share my story with others of overcoming Bulimia. My before and after story was featured in their transformation articles in the magazine. As I went on to compete in Nationals and placed 5th in my category, it was a very surreal moment for me. I felt in control, strong, and that I had finally found freedom from food.

It all seemed too good to be true, and, unfortunately, it was.

Chapter 5
The Rebound

Once the competition ended, I lost my focus, and I rebounded back into the habits that had dominated so much of my life; I was back to Bulimia. I remember the first time I had an episode I bargained with myself that it would just be the one time. I had been drinking and was not feeling well anyways so it was just for that reason.

However, it quickly made its way back into my everyday life and now it was worse.

I knew the steps I needed to take but I could not bring myself to get back into the dieting mode. I had spent so many months restricted that I deserved to have an extra bite, however every extra bite I ate led to a binge and a purge.

Since the structure of the competition was gone, I slipped back into eating whatever I wanted, whenever I wanted it – binging and purging all the time.

All competitors gain weight after a show. It is natural when you are on a highly restricted diet training intensely and often for months.

Dropping water, taking diuretics, and eliminating sodium are the final steps before a competition to create the overall look for stepping on stage. However, this all messes with your system and more importantly your head, as this becomes the physical barometer in which you hold yourself against, which is unattainable year round. Finding any sort of balance after a show takes a lot of work. Now many trainers offer a Reverse Dieting Programs to bring their clients back into a healthy weight range slowly. At that time, no one offered such support. I felt I had lost the balance that I had finally gained.

My rebound was very dark. I could not stop binging and purging. Then to add to the mix there were everyone's comments. I remember visiting stores as an Account Manager and being asked if I was pregnant, and one owner without hesitation asked me, "Why are you getting so fat now?" Once again I felt so much of my value was placed on how I looked. I wore the same thing almost every day, as I did not want to buy anything new at this size. I was disgusted with what I had fallen back into.

So my solution to this problem was to enter another fitness competition. I thought if I could compete again, then everything would be under control again. After this show I would not fall back into my cycle, or so I thought. However, to repeat a quote I'm sure we have all heard before, "The definition of insanity is doing the same thing over and over again and expecting different results." And, sure enough, after the second competition ended, I fell back into the same bulimic patterns. This pattern repeated itself several more times; with each competition charged with the same hope that I would gain control and not fall back into my horrible habit. Each time, I failed.

Chapter 6

The Turning Point

However, everything changed in the winter of 2008 when I found out I was pregnant with my daughter Mekaella. At that moment it no longer became just about me. I decided that I wanted to become a positive example to her. I started reflecting more and more on the decisions I had made in the past, and why I was continuing the same patterns. After much reflection I came to the conclusion that maybe it was my obsession with fitness all these years that caused my eating disorder.

So I stopped. I still worked out, but I decided not to worry about my diet anymore. I would eat "healthy" and make good choices, and just let go of whatever I thought I should look like or be -I would just accept myself. I spent the first several years of Mekaella's life not obsessing, however my day to day still revolved around food, even if it was in my head.

I still had the same triggers that caused my Bulimia. And no matter how much I wanted to stop, for myself and for my daughter, I had no control, especially when I consumed alcohol. With her father and I at constant odds I would drink, binge then purge. The feelings of failure were immense. Even though I tried to stop, it still continued. And to make it worse, I was now the heaviest I had ever been. I was out of shape. I was unhappy and I was struggling more than I ever had with food, diet and body issues. The only thing that was constant was my bulimia. I felt stuck and hopeless again.

Chapter 7
Sick and Tired

In the spring of 2011, Mekaella's father and I separated. As a single mother, I knew that now, more than ever, I had to be a strong and positive role model for my daughter. The constant battle with food and my relationship with my body was so exhausting and I so badly wanted peace but it seemed completely unattainable. I still could not stand in my "Why." I kept having episodes.

Until one day I was in the midst of a purge in the bathroom. I had the fan on and taps running to cover the sounds of my vomiting. The door was locked. (As a parent we all know that children will always just run in whenever it pleases them.) I heard a knock at the door and a little voice say, "Mommy, what are you doing?" At that moment I looked up, feeling my panic rise.

As I responded, "Nothing babe, be out in a second," I caught a glimpse of myself in the mirror. My eyes were watering from the purge, there was vomit and blood on my face and hand, my veins were bulging on my neck…. This was a sight I had experienced many, many times… but in that moment it was suddenly quite different.

My beautiful little 3-year-old was standing outside the door, her innocence, her love of everything and her body and mind not yet tainted by life. It was my responsibility to protect and love her. But I had none for myself.

I remember my eyes started tearing up and I started sobbing…

What was I doing?

How did this dominate so much of my life?

Why could I not love myself?

I was so sick and tired of being sick and tired.

I knew in that moment more than ever that I needed to get help. I wanted to stop; if not for me, then for her.

I had tried for countless years to stop and I thought I had tried everything. But what I did not know is my healing actually lied in confronting my bulimia, numbing, self hatred and weight issues head on.

I was finally ready to overcome my food demons, and figure out why I let these issues with food occupy so much of my precious time.

For once in my life I chose that moment. Not Monday, or the next birthday or holiday but that exact second to get real with who I was, who I wanted to be, the legacy I wanted to leave and what had to happen in that exact second to step into that.

I opened the door and scooped my beautiful little girl in my arms.

All these years I wanted the tenderness and love from others but would never allow it to for myself. In that moment as her arms wrapped tightly around my neck, I felt as though I was scooping little Aeryon in my arms. I began to view myself as my daughter, all these years of self-loathing and damage I had done. I was ready to let go of all of the perfectionism that I sought for so many years. My constant all-consuming search for the fill of boys, food, drugs, money, and alcohol clearly would never be enough. I could clearly see for the first time that I was responsible for my fill and what I needed was to fill myself with love. My story would not become *her* story.

The next several days I began to reflect back on the moments I had felt in control of my bulimia. It dawned on me that, oddly enough, it was when I was in fitness competition preparation.

Now of course, being in physique contest mode all the time was not possible. That's not the life I (or anyone) should live. It requires measuring your food, not going over an allotted carb, fat, or protein amount each day. It becomes obsessive, which was exactly what I was trying to step away from. In fact I could not remember a time in my life when I was not dieting. I realized in that moment I had to give up dieting, and step into a plan with flexibility and healthy eating.

However, what I did know is having structure was something that kept my bulimia at bay. Plus, the thought of my daughter dealing with an ED and body issues of her own strongly motivated me to finally find a solution. I then began to research other forms of treatment of bulimia. One of the more common practices now is to have set food throughout the day. Having your meals prepared enables consistency, so the mind cannot play games (ie. Well you did not eat today.... Or you ate that potato chip - you blew it). I looked at the extremes of the dieting I had practiced with the 'all or nothing'. For the first 21 days I was very careful and followed a healthy food plan, with no trigger foods or alcohol allowed. Then I started implementing more 80/20. By having the structure 80% of the time I felt ok with the 20% of fun foods.

The more I researched, the more I recognized the connection between my recovery and some of the steps I had taken unknowingly in regards to my competitive life.

Chapter 8
Reflection

As I began to reflect, I thought back to all the knowledge I had gathered over the years. I knew what to do to lose weight and feel healthy. I think most of us do. Choose whole foods, consume small meals and move our bodies. However, as with my clients I have worked with it was not that easy. The most powerful muscle we have is our brain and that is where my battle was often lost. In researching treatment for ED I stumbled upon Cognitive Behaviour Therapy (CBT) which is one of the most common used therapies (there are many forms that are also useful: Narrative, Strength, Solution, etc.) for this mental health illness.

Up to that point I never even comprehended that this was a mental health issue, so that was a huge revelation for myself in how I viewed my issues with food.

CBT was one treatment that seemed to appear in many of the articles I was reading. CBT had a huge impact on how I saw my dieting, bulimia, fitness competitions, and myself. Perhaps the most interesting discovery was the correlation between CBT's treatment of EDs and my own competitive preparation routine. I realized now why I felt so in control during competition preparation. My thoughts during prep were controlled and I felt empowered by my commitment, I had a plan and I was sticking to it. I had an end goal and knew that in following this I would achieve the result. Recognizing that my mindset was a crucial component in my healing I began to incorporate positive mantras and quotes that I still repeat to this day:

Daily Mantras:

- Don't take things personally.
- Let go of all attachment to the outcome.
- Stand in gratitude for every experience; it has created who I am today.
- Forgiveness is the greatest gift I can give myself.
- This has the meaning I attach to it.
- I am more than my body.
- The only constant in life is change.
- Everything is a result of a choice or action.
- Always listen to your gut, it is your guide.
- You are here for a reason…Your job is to figure out why…

So with that, I started planning and preparing my meals; in the beginning I was fairly structured, however after the first month I started using 80/20 rules weekly. During the week I had my meals planned and brought them with me to work and then on the weekend I could relax a bit and have some treats. I also steered away from processed starchy foods in the beginning, as I recognized these as my main triggers. I knew I had an issue with cake batter so with that I did not have cakes or pancake batter in the house for the first while. I started journaling and acknowledging how my stress had a direct effect on my desire to binge. I began to look at my need for control over situations and how I don't need things to be perfect but to accept them for what they are. I recognized that food had become a drug for me to numb and supress my feelings. I began to understand my eating disorder was rooted in emotional issues.

When experiencing stressful situations, I often felt a lack of control and to binge and purge often made me feel in control.

I also became aware of boredom, which often leads to overeating and then a purge.

This time things were different. I had a strong and solid "Why" and I was determined to succeed; much like I was when aiming for the stage. I had an end goal.

I wanted Fitness Sustainability. I had tried not dieting and training in the past and that did not work. Fitness has always been a huge part of my stress relief. By taking on mantras, support from friends and family, and journaling, I felt empowered, as I continued with my gym regime. This time I was mindful as to when Bulimic Aeryon would show up to critique a missed gym day or a relaxed workout. I chose nothing intense or over the top.

Slowly I began to "lose it" less. I was finally getting a grasp on my ED. I was not 100%, but now I knew the tools and strategies I could utilize. I removed triggers, stepped away if I felt anxiety arise, stood in my emotions, thought new empowering thoughts, and visualized myself healthy, whole and happy.

For the next year I used these tools and techniques. I felt free and in control without binging and purging.

Over the past 4-5 years I have been sharing my story, tools and techniques on a variety of stages and platforms. I no longer have the desire to step on stage in a bikini; that has been replaced with my desire to help others who struggle with their own food and body issues.

Although most do not suffer with an eating disorder, they can relate to the struggle with their body and food. The never ending up and downs of dieting, the "I'm not enough" dialogue that plays in our heads or the inability to connect and hold onto their "Why" when feeling challenged are a few of the issues that can show up. My story of low self worth led to issues with food. In the end I needed to learn to love myself first which finally led to change and a healthy pattern of eating.

I believe that starting a proactive conversation on eating disorders or issues with food is important. Those who are impacted can benefit from a positive environment rather than feeling shame for so long, as I did.

Using CBT and various techniques, I developed the following Tools and Strategies and that I use to this to this day. I am able to manage my Bulimia and negative body image. I incorporate my fitness lifestyle, partake in photo shoots and have found a love of this unique magical body that I call my own.

Chapter 9

My Why

When I had my Ahha moment in the bathroom all those years ago I came to the realization that unless I created massive change in my life, my daughter could follow my path of disordered eating and negative body image. The thought of her suffering created a very powerful "Why" that I used to propel me towards my goal of healing and letting go of unhealthy habits.

As a coach over the years I have found that most clients have a short term "Why." A short term goal such as a wedding or a vacation can provide the motivation to be disciplined and maintain healthy nutrition and fitness. However, it seems that to create lasting lifestyle change there needs to be a "Why" that is not only motivating but personally meaningful.

It has been said, "He who has a why can endure any how." Because I fully understood and knew where I wanted my life to go, I was prepared for any cost in relation to changing my belief system around food and myself. This meant doing the inner work emotionally, allowing past and present fears to be reconciled and accepting and setting up the structures in my daily life for the behavior changes. I was determined to find solutions each step of the way to meet the end goal of sustainable health for my daughter and myself.

There were adjustments along the way and I had to learn to forgive myself and let things go when I faltered. This was a big step in my healing process, as self-forgiveness and "letting go" were lessons I had to learn. The physical act of eating and purging for me is a metaphor of constant rejection of not only food. I would be faced with thoughts and feelings that would enter my body and "self" and I wanted them gone

- purged. Personally, there was a parallel to the removal and purging of food, to the removal and purging of thoughts and feelings. By learning to work through feelings and thoughts I learned to forgive myself and others, and to let things go.

Today, my "Why" is still the same. I want to be a positive role model for my daughter. However, I have realized that the greater reasons is to "Be" that person who honors self and the gift of a healthy body. It is about showing my daughter a healthy way to live, and more importantly, to live out gratitude and love for self and others. I hope that my story may not only speak to others, but give support in seeking to live in a healthy relationship with food our bodies, and family and friends.

Chapter 10
Planned Meals

When preparing for a competition I always had my meals with me to ensure I made correct choices. Once the prep was over though, I stopped planning, leading to lack of awareness of my food intake, eating when I should, and a possible subsequent binge. One of the things I found when I researched was the encouragement for those suffering with ED to have planned meals and bringing them with you. As time progresses, you can slowly ease into more of a relaxed space and flexibility, which is what I find works for me now. I make the time to have my meals and always have them with me. I'm not saying that I don't go out and eat or that I don't make poor choices sometimes. However, knowing that I have healthy food and snacks available is now part of my ongoing self-care support to achieve daily health sustainability.

I found that using higher Fat/Protein Macro's in my day to day meals enabled my triggers to dissipate, I had more energy and I felt better. All of my food triggers were starches. I never binged and purged on vegetables, fats or protein. It was always processed carbs.

I also began to become aware of negative thought processes I had created surrounding certain foods. Carbs were "bad" and in my Bulimic Aeryon's mind these were the cause behind my weight gain, and loss of control. In the beginning I chose to use carb sources that nourished me such as sweet potatoes, oatmeal, brown rice and quinoa when and if I needed them.

I had mental focus, clarity and was able to find balance. This new way eating was similar to my prep diet however I now had flexibility and finally was listening to my body cues of being hungry or full.

I began to connect with the energy that each food group gave me. Carbs were no longer were "bad" but rather an important resource for my body to recover and build. However, by tuning into how food made me feel I found if I had carbs earlier in the day I was exhausted by mid morning. So I began to look at having fats and protein instead for my first meals and snacks of the day.

I started a food journal with a new focus on why I was eating, how I was feeling emotionally and how the food made me feel physically, rather than counting calories. Intentionally noting how I was feeling, led to an awareness of my body responding best to certain foods.

After years of following this eating style I find what works for my body is higher protein, fats and vegetables. It is what my body operates best on. Depending on your body type this might not be what works for you. That is one of the reasons I believe having a food journal to take note of how different foods make you feel can be essential in finally figuring out what your body operates best with. When working with any plan I suggest keeping track of how your body responds to different Macros (Protein, Fats and Carbs). This is not counting calories anymore, this is about really connecting to your body and paying attention to what it needs and how it reacts.

In the beginning of my recovery I found I needed complete structure. Now I have far more flexibility to enjoy myself on any day. However, using the 80/20 rules and being tuned into what I feel best eating has been a key part in my creating lasting sustainability.

The idea behind the 80/20 rule is that 80% of the time you are following a healthy eating plan and 20% you let yourself have the freedom to go outside that. This can be done 80% of the week or 80% of your day. It is whatever works for you. Letting go of the dieting mentality has released the rigid set of rules that occupied so much of my relationship with food. I still believe that having structure and a system can provide the much needed support to keep the end objective in sight.

Below is an example of a 7 day plan.

	Day 1	Day 2	Day 3	Day 4 *Vegan Option*	Day 5	Day 6	Day 7
Breakfast	Shake: 1 scoop protein powder 1 tbsp nut butter (ex. almond/cashew/peanut) *Blend with unsweetened nut milk and ice*	½ cup oatmeal (measured dry) 2 hard boiled/poached/fired eggs	Egg white omelet: 1 cup egg whites ¼ cup shredded cheese Sautéed veggies Salsa Hot sauce	High Protein Toast: ½ avocado ½ cup kidney beans Fresh basil 2 slices "Little Big Bread" (Puree all ingredients together. Top toast and garnish with fresh tomato, salt and pepper)	Shake: 1 scoop protein powder 1 tbsp coconut oil *Blend with unsweetened nut milk and ice* (Optional add in: cinnamon/matcha powder/espresso shot)	2 slices "Little Big Bread" 2 hard boiled/poached/fried eggs	Shake: 1 scoop protein powder 1 tbsp hemp hearts *Blend with unsweetened nut milk and ice* (Optional add in: cinnamon/matcha powder/espresso shot)
Snack	*choose a snack option*	*choose a snack option*	*choose a snack option*	*choose a snack option*	*choose a snack option*	*choose a snack option*	*choose a snack option*
Lunch	1 protein choice 1oz feta cheese Mixed greens salad with your favorite veggies (ex. cucumber, cherry tomatoes, bell pepper, etc.) Light dressing	*Left over dinner from last night*	1 protein smoothie bowl	Mediterranean Lentil Salad: Cucumber Cherry tomato Red onion Bell pepper 1 cup cooked lentils Fresh Lemon Parsley	1 protein choice 1 carb choice (*left over from last night*) Mixed veggies	1 protein choice (*left over from last night*) Mixed greens salad with your favorite veggies Light dressing	*Left over dinner from last night*
Snack	*choose a snack option*	*choose a snack option*	*choose a snack option*	*choose a snack option*	*choose a snack option*	*choose a snack option*	*choose a snack option*
Dinner	1 protein choice 1 carb choice Mixed veggies Idea: Chicken soup *make an extra portion for tomorrows lunch*	1 protein choice Mixed greens salad with your favorite veggies ½ avocado Light dressing	1 protein choice 1 carb choice Mixed vegetables Idea: Tomato basil meat sauce over brown rice pasta	Tofu Fried Rice: 85g tofu Mixed veggies ½ cup rice 2 tbsp peanut sauce Tamari *cook extra rice for tomorrows lunch*	1 protein choice Mixed greens salad with your favorite veggies 1 oz feta Light dressing *cook an extra piece of protein for tomorrows lunch*	1 protein choice 1 carb choice Roasted/steamed vegetables Idea: Turkey burger with green bean "fries" *cook an extra portion of this meal to eat for lunch tomorrow*	1 protein choice Mixed veggies Idea: Chicken stir-fry

Food Options

Lean Protein
measured cooked

100g chicken breast
100g lean ground turkey
100g lean ground chicken
100g lean ground bison
100g lean ground beef
100g beef sirloin/tenderloin
100g cod
100g red snapper
100g basa
100g halibut
100g salmon
100g prawns
1 cup egg whites
1 can tuna

Carbs
measured cooked

100g sweet potato
100g yams
½ cup quinoa
½ cup brown rice
½ cup white rice
1 cup brown rice pasta
150g butternut squash
150g spaghetti squash
2 pieces sprouted bread
(Silver Hills - Little Big Bread)

Snacks

1 small apple with 1 tbsp nut butter
1 small apple with 3 oz cheese
Raw veggies with hummus
1 cup cottage cheese
1 cup Greek yogurt with ½ cup berries
1 banana
24 almonds/walnuts/cashews
2 rice cakes with 1 tbsp nut butter
2 rice cakes with ⅕ avocado
1 mini bag smart pop popcorn
1 protein bar
2 hard boil eggs
1 grapefruit
1 cup berries
Steamed edameme beans with sea salt
Celery with 1 tbsp nut butter

Smoothie:
1 scoop protein
1 cup berries
1 tbsp nut butter
Unsweetened almond milk
Ice

Chapter 11
Trigger Foods

During my quest to heal I began to look honestly at my trigger foods and made the decision not to have them in my house. For me, the big triggers were popcorn and cake batter. The central issue for me was to stay away from any processed starchy foods. This explains why whole foods higher in fats, protein, and vegetables worked well during my recovery and as I transitioned to routinely making healthy choices without lapsing to negative eating patterns.

As with other addictions we have the option to not engage in situations that involve the substance or vice. However, with food addicts, and people with Bulimia, Anorexia, and Binge Eating issues, that option is not viable. We have to find a way to manage because food is all around us and we need it to survive. We can't just quit eating and we can't eliminate 'people who eat" from our lives. Often, depending where you are in your recovery, this can seem like an unattainable goal.

Establishing guidelines surrounding food creates safety and structure. Understanding that certain foods can trigger me, I chose to not to have them in my house. I know I won't binge on vegetables or healthy snacks.

The nutrition guideline not only left me feeling healthy, but a great sense of pride and accomplishment. In retrospect it was a huge a huge 'overcoming' moment/time. To borrow from an old spiritual – We shall overcome- 'I shall overcome!!' I had overcome my impulses and desire to drown emotions and negative patterns of eating.

I believe celebration of these moments is important. Sharing with family and friends provides milestones along the way, recognizing and reinforcing the monumental shifts and changes we make to our day to day living.

The next 21 days I followed a similar food plan which yielded the same results and with each 21 day cycle my self esteem and self discipline grew. I am happy to report, there was an unexpected bonus. As I shared earlier I could not have my trigger foods in the house. If I wanted popcorn I would go to the movie theatre order a small one and enjoy it. However, over time, the obsession for snacks, popcorn, and cake batter lessened! I could have them in my home without controlling me. This was my experience and how it will be for others re-introducing trigger foods depends on each person's circumstance.

Chapter 12
No Scale

For a long period of time, the scale dominated my day, mood and thoughts. Several years ago I made the promise to no longer use the scale.

For some people, the scale can be a positive tool to track their fitness goals. However, for me, the number that would appear determined my worthiness. I vividly remember stripping down to nothing first thing in the morning, and then factoring in how much water I had drank, if I had gone to the bathroom etc. A number that in all honesty never brought me any happiness or fulfillment consumed my life. It was not unlikely that I would step on the scale 3-4 times a day each time praying that I even dropped an ounce. Countless mornings I felt great in my body and then once I weighed myself it was never the number I hoped for and lead to immediate depression and judgement.

The scale may work for you, but if it causes you to equate a number to your self worth as I experienced, then you may want to move away from the 'Number Monitor' as I did. It is all about learning to stand in self-love and removing anything that allows a negative narrative (that I labelled my 'Nasty Girl') to have a voice.

Here are 5 Empowering Ways to Track Your Fitness without the use of a scale.

- Keep a Feeling journal. How is your energy, strength, sleep?
- Take progress pictures

- Measure your Hips, Thighs or Biceps.
- Have a strength based fitness marker you use (PB Squat, Deadlift, Sprint etc.)
- Count your active minutes on an app or device.

Chapter 13

Journaling

When I became aware of the connection to numbing my emotions with food I began to realize how disconnected I was from my own body and hunger cues. One of the tools I began to use was a food journal. In the past I had recorded my food intake as a method to add up calories and punish myself for eating "Bad Foods."

Journaling in this way created a whole new dimension in my journey as it deepened my self-understanding in relation to food and my body. The journal provided a way to make sense of the healing process of my journey. The chart recording what I ate, when, how much, and my feelings, especially when there was an urge to binge, caused me to step back and reflect. Giving language to how I was feeling and making associations was very powerful. With identifying emotions and what life was bringing my way, I made different choices from the past. My chart and my journal were key tools in my journey for not only self-understanding but practical change and new patterns of living.

On this chart I recorded the following.

1. Time of day, was it morning, mid day or evening? How did the time of day connect with my desire to eat? Was I alone or bored? I began to examine the connection to filling time or space with food.
2. Which food I went for? Is a food that evokes a memory or comfort?

3. Quantity, how much did I consume? Did I just have enough to satisfy my craving or did it become a full out binge?
4. Was I hungry before and full after? Bringing awareness to my physical cues.
5. What were my thoughts, feelings mood and energy? Was I stressed, sad, lonely, depressed, overwhelmed?
6. Lastly what was my satiety level from 1-10 once I was done eating? Did this satisfy my desire to eat? Or was I left feeling empty, depressed and wanting more.

By bringing awareness to when and why I was eating it created a connection to my body and emotions I had not yet experienced. Food journaling has been a very powerful tool to step into awareness.

Below is the Food and Feeling Chart used to create awareness to why we are eating and the connection to our emotions.

Food & Feelings

Date: _____
Day: ☐ Mon   ☐ Tue   ☐ Wed   ☐ Thu   ☐ Fri   ☐ Sat   ☐ Sun

Time	Food	Quantity	Hungry Before?	Full After?	Thought, feelings, Mood, Energy	Satiety level (1-10)

Chapter 14

Support

It is valuable in everyday life to have a network of family and friends who offer support and feedback, and this is especially true regarding challenging food issues. For meaningful change to occur, I needed to be open and honest, even though I felt vulnerable. I began the recovery and healing process with the love and acceptance of family and friends in an atmosphere of non-judgement. Finding a network of support is a big first step, and that can include professional resources or organizations.

There is a silence around eating disorders that I have witnessed. Many are 'silently suffering,' feeling shame and guilt for patterns of eating where there seems to be no escape. Over the past several years, men and women in their late 30's and 40's have confided with me that even after a few decades, they are still struggling with disordered eating habits and negative self body issues.

They are working mothers and wives, husbands and fathers who portray that they seemingly have their lives together (Perfectionism). Admitting such a dark secret is not something they are willing to do.

Recently a lady confessed that she had been married for 25 years and that her husband had no idea she was still purging weekly. She informed me that she was not interested in seeking professional help but she wanted to be informed of the strategies I used in dealing with my food issues. This overwhelming fear of judgement can keep us in secrecy, create isolation and further perpetuate the ongoing silence.

However, what I have learned is that a shoulder to lean on or talk to is not that far away and it does not need to be someone directly in your life.

There are many helpful organizations and Food Behaviour Coaches that provide support. A good place to start for support is an organization such as NEDIC (National Eating Disorder Information Centre).

True healing started when I let go of the idea of being perfect and being okay with feeling vulnerable. Then I surrounded myself as much as possible with support! It does take a village to start a new path of eating and living!!

Chapter 15

Anxiety

I never thought I suffered from anxiety. In fact I thought I was the opposite. As an extrovert and naturally outgoing person I had never experienced what I interpreted anxiety to be.

However, as I began to work towards my recovery I started to reflect on my physical reaction surrounding food and my binging behaviour. Right before I am triggered, my heart rate increased, my mind raced and I felt overwhelmed with the urge to eat.

Once I'm completely immersed and the binge commenced, the intensity to consume as much as possible in one sitting was overwhelming. I can best describe it as frantic. This sensation of losing complete control with food waved over me like a warm blanket, I felt for a moment, almost joyful.

Then as the sensation of feeling full (uncomfortably full) would be overwhelming there was a complete 180° switch. That joy shifted to extreme panic as I became desperate to purge and gain control again.

What I have been able to do is to stop, pay attention to, and recognize the anxiety. I feel it showing up in different times. Pausing, stepping back and connecting with the stresses that I am trying to supress with the numbing of food, has now become a focal point. I ask myself what is my anxiousness about? Is it issues in my personal life? Family? Career? Can I take the time now or later to share this with someone or look at this differently? What works best for me to reflect on this issue? I need to breathe deeply and tell myself I am ok!

Breathing has been a wonderful tool that I can do anywhere. I simply inhale through my mouth for 5, hold for 7, then exhale for 9. I repeat affirmations and stand in gratitude and repeat this 5 times.

Physical exercise is also another wonderful stress and anxiety relief tool. Even creating a 20 min window each day to move your body not only releases endorphins but can create a shift your mental state. It does not need to be hours in a gym. Playing with your children or going for a walk to appreciate the gift of nature are wonderful ways to move your body and create moments that matter.

I have researched and rely on some valuable natural products. Fish Oil, Ashwaganda, 5HTP, B Vitamins, Theanine, Gaba and Vitamin D. These products aid in anxiety, mood and relaxation. Many of these also help support the adrenals, which I touched on earlier in chapter one. I have found that these products lessen my anxiety and increase feelings of relaxation.

However, if you find your anxiety is overwhelming I advise going to see your medical practitioner and seek their advice.

Chapter 16
Affirmations

I have found using positive affirmations in my day-to-day can help release stressors that are causing anxiety. We may not have control over all the circumstances in our lives but we can control our response. Creating personal, meaningful affirmations that are repeated throughout the day can be proactive for a positive mindset, shifting our reaction to negative events.

I appreciate the Oprah Winfrey statement "That which you focus on expands." Becoming aware of our thoughts and how they create feelings and actions is imperative in shifting our relationship with ourselves.

To create your own affirmation use the following steps.

1. Think of a thought pattern your Nasty internal voice repeats that does not serve you. It can be from your childhood or something that you still have deep attachment too.

    For example: "I am not enough"

2. Write a statement that counters that old belief that no longer serves you. Begin your affirmation with "I" as this creates identity, which is a powerful motivator for change. Your new statement must be emotionally charged with feeling and in the present moment in time.

    For example: "I am worthy, valuable and loved"

3. Place that new affirmation in places that you will see it daily. I use Post it notes on my mirrors, day timer and in my car. You might even have it on the home screen of your phone. In

order we rewire your limiting thoughts this must be practiced daily.

There are many apps and books on Affirmations available if you find it challenging to come up with a list of your own. In the remainder of the chapter I have included some of the Affirmations from my Mind, Body, Spirit program.

1

Today is a new day.
It holds possibilities and potential.
It is mine to create.
What happened yesterday is the past.
I let it go.
I have the ability to overcome whatever life brings me.
I am luminous.
I am blessed.
I am grateful for who I am.
I love my body.
I shall focus on the good in my life.
I am now creating my life exactly how I want.

2

Good Morning Beautiful.
This will be a blessed day.
All my experiences are creating the person I am destined to be.
Life loves and supports me!
I am a magnet for miracles.
I am strong.
I am powerful.
I am enough.
There is enough time for everything.
This will be a blessed day.

3

Today I am full of energy.
I feel empowered and in control.
I can handle whatever life brings me.
I trust my instincts.
I follow my intuition.
I let go of what no longer serves me.
I stand in gratitude.
I am exactly where I am supposed to be.
I am happy and blessed.
I love myself.

4

As I take a deep breath.
I feel my lungs expand with sweet air.
I am blessed with this life.
I breathe in gratitude and love.
I exhale my fears and anger.
I know the Universe supports me .
I trust my journey.
I am magical.
I am unique.
I here for a reason.

5

I trust myself.
I trust my body.
I listen to my intuition.
I am on the right path.
I am loved.
My heart is open.
My intentions are pure.
I am not scared.
My inner self always knows what to do.
All is well and I am safe.

6

I am Brave.
I am Smart.
I am Strong.
I am Beautiful.
I am one of a kind.
I am a gift.
I am a blessing.
I am a piece of the Universe.

7

Food is not my enemy.
I am in control.
My body is efficient.
I eat when I am hungry.
I always have enough.
All things are possible.
Everything will come in perfect time.
I have no fear.
I make a difference in the world.
I trust my inner light.
I am loved.
I am supported.
My body is healthy.
I am blessed.

Chapter 17
Tapping

Tapping, also known as EFT (Emotional Freedom Technique), is another resource that has been beneficial whenever I am feeling anxious. This might be a strategy, choosing to investigate professional resources in this method. I have found this similar to acupuncture in that it utilizes the body's energy meridian points. By tapping these points with your fingers you are tapping into your own body's energy and healing power. Using the combination of your index and your middle fingertips, either hand works.

While tapping on the pressure points below you repeat affirmations either under your breath or in your head.

Here is an example of one of my Tapping affirmations;

> *"Even though I have fear of food, I deeply and completely accept myself. Even though I get anxiety with food, I deeply and completely accept myself. Even though I have chased perfection, I deeply and completely accept and love myself."*

TH = Top of Head
EB = Eye Brow
SE = Side of the Eye
UE = Under the Eye
UN = Under the Nose
Ch = Chin

CB = Collar Bone
UA = Under the Arm
WR = Wrists

EFT Tapping Points

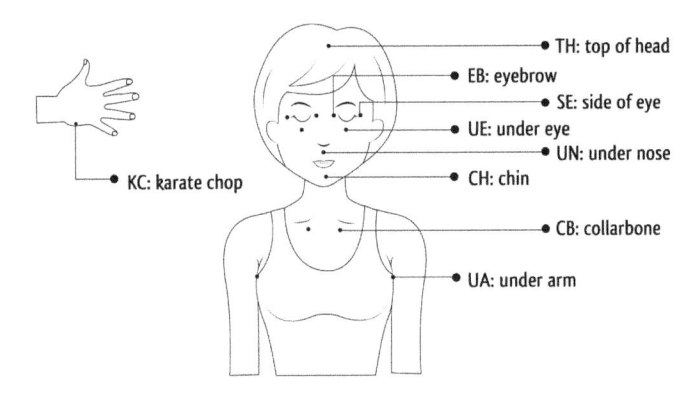

- TH: top of head
- EB: eyebrow
- SE: side of eye
- UE: under eye
- UN: under nose
- CH: chin
- KC: karate chop
- CB: collarbone
- UA: under arm

Chapter 18

Breathing

During stressful times or anxiety attacks our heart rate and breathing rapidly increases. This can lead to hyperventilation. In creating awareness we can connect to our breath and can shift back to a more relaxed state. I often found that with food and overeating, as my urge to binge appeared I would feel incredibly anxious.

Mindful breathing has been an essential tool that I have used for years in numerous situations to manage my physical symptoms of stress. By focusing on the exhale of each breath as I detailed below, a sense of calm and control outweighs the anxiety. This has been for me, one of the most effective grounding exercises for stress.

Below are 3 different breathing techniques I use to help with stress and anxiety.

1. Inhale through my mouth for 5, hold for 7, and then exhale for 9. Repeat 5-10 times.
2. Placing one hand on my chest and the other on my belly, I take a deep breathe in through my nose and ensure my diaphragm is expanding. Repeat 5-10 times.
3. Begin by taking a long, slow inhale through the nose then proceed by powerfully exhaling from the lower belly out your mouth making a "Whoosh" sound until you feel all the breathe has left your body. Repeat 5-10 times.

just ♡ breathe

Chapter 19
Exercise

Physical exercise has been vital for me as a stress relief and reducing anxiety. For most of my life my relationship with fitness was based on guilt or punishment for food I had consumed. As I worked though my healing I began to look at fitness in a different context. It became my way of giving thanks for my health and ability to move my body without pain and suffering.

As I shifted by expectations of "Fitness" I slowly stopped spending hours in the gym. Playing with my daughter or going for a walk appreciating nature provides ways to move my body and create moments that matter. By creating a 20 min window each day for movement, this not only releases endorphins but can create a shift in my mental state.

If you are a person who does not like the gym I suggest looking at activities you loved as a child and try taking them up again. There are so many outlets for exercise and it is worth the time and effort to find one that resonates with you.

After we discover the sports, exercise, or movement that gets us up and going, we need to make a plan. If for example a dance or yoga class is motivating, then commit to a plan several times a week.

Below is an example of a mini circuit that my daughter and I do together during the commercial breaks while watching our family program. We do 3 different exercises 10 times during commercial breaks and repeat it each break. We call this You Tube video series "Commercial Break Workout." I believe it is important to include our children. We model healthy living, demonstrating the importance of time together and exercise.

I have learned to live in a deeper appreciation of my body and health. The added benefit has been gaining a sense of freedom from the need to spend extreme amounts of time in fitness, and the inevitable guilt that would follow. I am learning to live in gratitude rather than guilt.

Commercial Break Workout:

> Workout 1:
>> 10 Jumping Jacks
>> 10 Chair Dips
>> 10 Crunches
>
> Workout 2:
>> 10 Chair Squats
>> 10 Pushups
>> 10 Jumping Jacks
>
> Workout 3
>> 10 Pop Squats
>> 10 Air Punches
>> 10 sec Plank

Please note: If you find any exercise painful then you need to acknowledge that your body is speaking to you and modify it or preform a new exercise.

Chapter 20
Supplements

Over the years I have researched and relied on some valuable natural products to help with my anxiety, mood and relaxation. Some of these also help support the adrenals, which I touched on earlier in Chapter one. I have found that incorporating these into my daily regime at various times have definitely been an added benefit.

Fish Oil:

Omega 3 plays a huge role in brain health, heart health and inflammation. Research has shown that EPA and DHA, which are, are the main fatty acids in Omega 3 and contribute to lowering anxiety. However, since the body cannot produce Omega 3 we must source it from our diet. Salmon, Sardines, Mackerel plus Omega 3 supplements are all viable sources.

Ashwaganda:

Ashwaganda has been used for centuries in Ayurvedic medicine and is known as an adaptogen. Adaptogen is defined as a natural substance considered to help the body adapt to stress and a normalizing effect on body processes. Research has shown that by taking Ashwaganda it can reduce the stress hormone cortisol by 28%. This supplement also helps with insomnia, stabilizes mood, reduces depression, assists with weight loss and has no side effects.

B Vitamins:

B Vitamins can be sourced from liver, meats, whole grains, legumes and potatoes, bananas, molasses and nutritional yeast to name a few.

Taking a B complex vitamin is beneficial for stress, anxiety, PMS, balancing out depressive moods and healthy cell production.

GABA:

Gaba is an amino acid that is produced in our bodies with 2 primary functions; it regulates muscle tone and acts as a neurotransmitter. Gaba can relieve anxiety by exerting a calming effect. Mackeral, Wheat Germ, Beef liver, broccoli, brown rice and almonds are all GABA boosting foods. Lemon Balm and L-Theanine are two supplements that contain Gaba compounds.

These are just a few of the supplements I have found effective in dealing with my anxiety surrounding food. However, before you undergo any new supplement regime, I recommend that you seek medical advice from your practitioner.

References:

https://academic.oup.com/omcr/article/2015/3/244/1448354 https://www.psychologytoday.com/ca/blog/evolutionary-psychiatry/201111/fish-oil-and-anxiety

Kulkarni, S. K., and Ashish Dhir. "Withania somnifera: an Indian ginseng." Progress in neuro-psychopharmacology and biological psychiatry 32, no. 5 (2008): 1093-1105.

https://www.mayoclinic.org/diseases-conditions/depression/expert-answers/vitamin-b12-and-depression/faq-20058077

https://www.ncbi.nlm.nih.gov/pubmed/20655491

Chapter 21
Mindfulness

As I touched on in the previous chapters, awareness has become a huge part of my healing. What does it mean to be aware? It is commonly understood as trying to be "in the moment." This requires effort!! We rush through our days, and with good reason; we are busy. Often life seems to resemble a hamster on a wheel running in circles. Another challenge of day to day living is social media. It shapes us to be reactive, solution focused and having easy swift answers.

An unexpected outcome of my eating disorder was the necessity to pay attention, reflect and ponder how I was thinking, feeling and acting. Journaling, being in conversation with others, charting responses to how certain foods made me feel replacing negative self talk with positive affirmations, are a few of the changes that I have shared in my story. I moved from a place of reaction to a deeper response and self caring and love.

Mindful eating has been another step in my journey. I was 'aware' years ago that while I ate, I was almost unconscious of the food I was consuming. Being 'mindful' while eating, is a difficult task with bulimia, binge eating or other disordered eating habits. Practicing mindfulness has been essential for me as I have learned to be deliberate and intentional in what I am eating, focusing on health, rather than substituting my emotions for food.

I have learned to stop and taste food. The next step was to actually enjoy what I was eating! To be present and in the moment while eating, I have made the following purposeful efforts:

1. I no longer stand in front of the refrigerator mindlessly eating or snack while cooking.
2. I eat with my family and use a plated meal.
3. I pay attention to the color, taste, texture, and appearance.
4. I chew slowly (32 times is the recommended number) which not only helps digestion but in taking 20 minutes to finish your meal, the brain is signaled that the stomach is full.
5. I take a moment to give thanks for my food; by appreciating my meal before me it creates connection to what I am about to eat.
6. We have created mealtime as sacred and an opportunity to connect and listen. No matter how big your family is, connecting with each other can greatly improve your health and relationships.

I have found value in the use of meditation to centre myself and get connected to my body. Starting or ending the day with a 5 min meditation is an effective tool for creating a space of releasing stress and being calm.

Learning the art of connecting with my breath and my body has been beyond powerful, especially those moments when Bulimic Aeryon shows up. Each evening I do a meditation as I prepare to sleep and each morning I practice visualization with a daily '5 Things I am Grateful For.' If and when negative thoughts arise I catch myself and shift my focus to gratitude. Even if it is the smallest thing, I always have something I am grateful for.

As researchers have shown, the mind/body connection is very powerful. Visualization is used around the world in relation to many areas of our life such as competing in sports, power over addictions, and dealing with illness.

Simply by connecting to breath, feeling our heartbeat, recognizing the power and magic that makes us human has created a way to step out of the food and body obsession. By taking a moment each day to stand in gratitude and self-reflection opens a new landscape from which we can view our lives.

I no longer let food have power over me, I am in control of my destiny, I am aware and connected. In creating a mindful connection to my body and food I am able to stand in greater appreciation for the journey that has unfolded in my life. I am not a victim but a designer/artist in my life. I refuse to let my negative mind chatter, or disempowering language control me anymore. I am mindful, I am now awakened to my own power.

Creating a weekly list of Gratitude is a great reference tool when we get stuck in moments that can be challenging.

Weekly Gratitude Chart

Monday _____
1. _____
2. _____
3. _____

Tuesday _____
1. _____
2. _____
3. _____

Wednesday _____
1. _____
2. _____
3. _____

Thursday _____
1. _____
2. _____
3. _____

Friday _____
1. _____
2. _____
3. _____

Saturday _____
1. _____
2. _____
3. _____

Sunday _____
1. _____
2. _____
3. _____

Chapter 22
Goal Setting

Creating goals in most areas of my life was an important practice. When I made the obvious decision to implement goal setting around my relationship with food, body image and bulimia, I found the process I needed to remain focused.

Setting **SMART** (specific, measurable, attainable, relevant and time-bound) goals is exactly what I needed to make my recovery a reality.

Here is how it worked for me:

1. Make sure your goals are clear, specific and measurable.
2. Make sure you aim high and set goals that challenge you.
3. Make sure that you are rationally and emotionally committed to achieving your goals.
4. Monitor your progress by developing a weekly and quarterly review process to help you stay on track.
5. Consider the complexity of the tasks demanded by your goals and chunk them into smaller tasks when appropriate. Also, be sure to make time for learning, development and growth.

There have been countless studies that have shown that those who write down their goals using these systems are more likely to achieve them.

Further to the major goal, and strategies, there were specific goals that I knew I wanted to accomplish to be healthy in mind, body and emotions/soul. The overall life goal was that I would live a healthy life and be a positive example to my daughter.

In my relationship to food I wrote that I would no longer binge and purge. I would recognize when bulimic Aeryon showed up and instead of resorting to food to numb I would determine different methods to relieve my stress. I analyzed specific goals that I knew I had to accomplish to be healthy: mind, body and soul. My top goal was not settling for an unhealthy life and instead being a positive example for my daughter.

In regards to my ED recovery, it was essential. I wrote a list that I wanted to accomplish daily, weekly, monthly and annually. Making it through one day without a binge or episode is how I started my journey. Each day as I made it through I accomplished one step closer to my final goal. Setting small, achievable goals every day helped me to move forward, and feel in control of my destiny. Reaching one day without a binge is often the first step. Offering myself empathy and compassion along the way is very important. I began to appreciate that it was learning to live with those qualities was my end goal! If I could accept that I needed to be flexible within my goals, and that life can happen, then I was making an accomplishment. To replace the perfectionism that had been part of my eating disorder with perfection related to goals would only continue my inner negative dialogue. I was learning self love with flexibility in setting my goals.

Setting goals was a very pragmatic practical process! First, I wrote my goal of no longer binging and purging. This action was a first step to recognize when my bulimic Aeryon showed up and instead of resorting to food to numb, I would look at different methods to relieve my stress. I analyzed a list of specific goals that I knew I had to accomplish to be healthy: mind, body and soul. My main goal was to only settle for a healthy life and being a positive example to my daughter.

Here is a simple example of using the S.M.A.R.T technique for Goal Setting. Creating a Goal, establishing your WHY and plan of action to take you towards your desired result.

Goal Digger

Goal	ACTION STEPS
	1.
	2.
	3.
	4.
	5.
WHY THIS IS IMPORTANT	

Goal	ACTION STEPS
	1.
	2.
	3.
	4.
	5.
WHY THIS IS IMPORTANT	

Goal	ACTION STEPS
	1.
	2.
	3.
	4.
	5.
WHY THIS IS IMPORTANT	

Chapter 23

Forgiveness

In the past, I would beat myself up after a binge and purge. It would often take me down a dark path that supported more unhealthy behaviour. It was a vicious cycle of thoughts, feelings and behaviours. Because I felt a failure, it seemed that everything was lost and I could only tailspin. Now I understand it for what it is- just a single, isolated episode. It no longer defines me or owns me.

I am human, and I will make many mistakes in my life. Letting go of trying to be perfect, I have learned to embrace the values of self-compassion and forgiveness. This has diminished so much of the power that binge eating held over me. I would get so wrapped up in an episode that it would consume me. The internal dialogue was one of shame and defeat. The perfectionist part of myself operated in extremes, as it would be an all or nothing attitude. The thought of messing up and letting things pass by was unthinkable.

I had the mentality that because I had already failed, I rationalized that I might as well keep going in failure.

Other ways I began to heal and offer myself forgiveness was looking at ways in which I could give back. Having an eating disorder is a very self-absorbed illness. How could this have been positive?

I wanted a life that was about having time and energy to think about how I could support others, and make a difference.

How I could help others?

Speak to those who needed support?

Be okay with sharing my story?

Be vulnerable and share my illness?

I wanted to step outside the realm of "Me Me Me." I learned that supporting others was the biggest privilege for me, and though I liked to think I was helping, I received the most benefit sharing and learning in a caring community.

Chapter 24
CBT Therapy

Cognitive Behavioural Therapy is a very powerful tool that is commonly used for the treatment of Eating Disorders. There are many different types of Therapies that assisted in my healing; Narrative, Strength, Solution based to name a few. However, the use of CBT was my original choice, and the one I still work with most to this day.

Cognitive Behaviour Therapy focuses on patterns of thinking that are distorted and the beliefs that are the root cause of irrational thinking. CBT aims to incorporate psychodynamic and behavioural therapies in help to relieve symptoms that someone may be experiencing. The key concept revolves around the idea that thoughts and feelings are tied with behaviour. Therefore, the goal of CBT is to help individuals learn that while they cannot control every aspect of their day to day environment, they are able to gain control of how circumstances in their surrounding are interpreted and managed.

Learning how to change the constant thoughts of unworthiness and shame while also feeling helpless and isolated, and in turn binging and purging, requires self 'work.' Understanding how we create everything with our thoughts is not only empowering but practical as we learn to take control of what our lives look like. How that looks for each person is different: seeking support professionally, and/or with other community resources.

I began to view the Nasty thoughts that dominated my head as just thoughts. I made the choice to not let them have power by stepping into new thoughts of gratitude and /or self-affirmation. I carried a small notepad where I recorded new positive thoughts so I could refer to those when I was struggling. I found that by using these tools I was able to let negative thoughts go. Just as I needed discipline in the area of nutrition and fitness, I needed to apply diligence in my daily thoughts and attitudes. It did not happen immediately, but with small steps, and again being kind to myself, I observed I was referring less to my notepad. Over time, the negative thought pattern lessened and new patterns emerged.

There was a freedom I felt in 'conquering' these thoughts that can only be described as 'finding my bliss' (a phrase coined by Joseph Campbell.) Every day is not 'blissful' and perfect, and I do not pretend to have all the answers. I have though, broken negative patterns that the 'nasty' voice held in my brain. With many inspiring women role models who have chosen the path that may require work and discipline, I see the rewards of living in your best as the years pass by.

Chapter 25

Nasty Girl

One of the strategies that I have used in gaining control over the negative mind chatter or the Nasty Girl has been identifying when her voice shows up. We all have that internal voice that causes doubt, fear, tells us we are not enough, too fat etc. This is the voice that holds us back from believing in ourselves, for taking the initiative to pursue the job of our dreams or being open to love and relationships. This negative mindset is often related to experiences from childhood whether they be isolated events or neglect and abuse. I carried negative chatter from my childhood into teen and adult years. For those with serious trauma whether physical or psychological, therapeutic support may be necessary.

A strategy I have found useful in dealing with this constant negative mind chatter was giving this inner voice a name and certain personality traits that I believed to be less desirable. By creating a a persona for this Nasty Girl I was able to take away some of the power she held over me. In my day to day I would never let someone bully me and speak to me in such a manner. I would never even think of speaking like this to my daughter, a friend, family member or even someone I did not like. Yet for some reason I let this Nasty Girl dominate so much of my life. Because of my disordered eating, my negative voice was very prominent in my daily thoughts. I believed what she was saying. Finally, I owned my power and took away the voice of the Nasty girl when I identified her as just a bully in my mind.

Stopping her voice was intentional work with continued journaling, note taking, affirmations, meditation, and positive supportive conversations with my network of family and friends.

With more reflection concerning this Nasty voice, I found some further helpful personal insights. That voice came from a place of hurt. Maybe she was the little girl wanting attention, to have a hug, and told she was special. Again, I needed a response of compassion and empathy for that part of me that had given voice and taken residence in my mind a long time ago. As I have shared, if we can respond with love and self-care to what shows up in our lives, there are small victories that lead to where we want to be, and become.

"I see you….I know you are hurting and I no longer let you control my thoughts, feelings and actions"…I am able to let it go….

Change the Narrative

Disempowering Narrative?: _____
_____

3 New Empowering Narratives:
1. _____
2. _____
3. _____

Disempowering Narrative?: _____
_____

3 New Empowering Narratives:
1. _____
2. _____
3. _____

Disempowering Narrative?: _____
_____

3 New Empowering Narratives:
1. _____
2. _____
3. _____

Chapter 26
Bulimia My Friend

One of the most significant moments in my healing was coming to the realization that my Bulimia was actually my friend.

I know this sounds absurd. How could something that negatively impacted my life in so many ways actually be viewed as my friend? My 20+ year battle resulted in worsened eyesight, a mouth full of implants and crowns from the stomach acid, having to wear a heart monitor from fainting, and the ongoing obsession with food, negative body image and fitness as punishment for the guilt I felt around food. This all required years to overcome.

What I understand now is that when I am stressed, upset or not in tune with my needs, my bulimic Aeryon shows up. She shows up with a little nudge for me to get still and pay attention to something I am trying to stuff. She is not as loud as she was in my past, where her "presence" meant a prod to binge. I don't fall into that game anymore. I take the nudge as a reminder to get a little still, to check in with myself and offer myself some empathy. I journal, call a friend, or practice some tapping or meditation. These actions nourish and bring me calm and peace, because I acknowledge and feel my emotions. Learning to stand in my body and connect with what I am feeling, I no longer need to numb nor want to numb with food.

Are there circumstances where a different perspective can make things positive for you?

Do cravings, urges, addictions often show up when you need to be centred as I experienced?

Instead of ignoring of falling in to a negative pattern, can you try some positive strategies that bring you to a new experience?

The call to Bulimia in my life is now a call to pay attention to, and love Aeryon. If you are suffering from addictions, the call is to find support resources and strategies you need to love yourself.

Chapter 27

Creating a New Story

In life we are often a result of the story that has happened to us and that we have created based on our experiences. For myself my earliest memory is at the school yard when I was 5 and the kids were chasing me around making fun of me and calling me fat. Then to sexual abuse, always feeling "Not enough." Being a pre-teen homeschooled because of the constant bullying in school, to my parents struggling to do what's right in regards to their daughters weight, to being told if I could just loose "10 more lbs, I'd be perfect," the list goes on and on.

These layers of hurt complied over the years and brought me to where I am today. Yes, I did end up going down some very dark paths looking to be filled including boys, drugs and food.

Truthfully, when my daughter knocked on the door that day I could have carried on my unhealthy relationship with myself and food. I did not need to make a change, however one of the most profound things I have recognized is I always have a choice. Always.

I can let my past continue to hover over me like a dark cloud as my excuse to not step fully into who I am destined to be. Or I can make a decision to make a massive shift in my destiny.

Everything in life is about choices. Sometimes circumstances happen that are beyond our control. We still have a choice in our reaction, if we are going to let the layers of hurt and shame hold us down or build us up. We all have our pain, hurt and disappointment. The real magic lies in what we decide to do with it.

I cannot change my past, but I can most certainly change the future. I made a decision that day, and it has not always been easy. My Nasty Girl still shows up, I still struggle at times.

But the only reason my past has a future today is because I bring it here everyday. I made the decision to see it for what it was; events that happened, but I get the choice in what I do with it now.

I'm creating a new powerful story with my body and food…

Chapter 28

Bulimia to Balance

What I have learned through my journey with food and body issues is that the most important thing I had to control was not food or exercise but the daily thoughts that inhabit my mind.

Managing my Eating Disorder is similar to the organization I use in my work, life, home, and my relationships. I know by using certain guidelines, I produce the results I need.

At some point things are beyond my control and in those moments, I've learned to forgive myself. I stop, take a breath, and remember that I am not perfect, and I don't need to be.

I have learned to be aware of my triggers, what they are and how to deal with them. Using supplementation and meditation have all become an important part of my ongoing healing. Letting go of the idea of perfectionism and aiming to be my best self, moment-to-moment, has freed me from unrealistic expectations. Because truthfully, in the end, that is all I have.

This story began with my younger self, desiring to look, and be looked at, in a certain way. This resulted in a 20+ year, fearful and possessive relationship with food, and a distrustful relationship with my body and myself.

I'm not saying that I still don't have anxious moments when it comes to food, or my body, or even certain social situations. However, I try to keep things in perspective, take it one day at a time, and sometimes one hour at a time.

I now know the value of being kind to myself, and to realistically confront my own weaknesses, by learning to see my true strengths.

And finally, most importantly, I have learned that I can be the positive role model that my daughter needs, and deserves, only when I am honest with who I am.

I have finally found a path from Bulimia to Balance….

About the Author
Aeryon Ashlie

Aeryon Ashlie has been involved in the Health and Fitness industry in a variety of capacities over the past 20 years. Since she was a young girl, Aeryon struggled with negative body and self image issues. This mindset was expressed as a teen into excessive exercise and a variety of disordered eating patterns, with bulimia being the primary choice. Aeryon lived the experience of shame, guilt, and negative daily mind chatter as she struggled for years to overcome the control of disordered eating. Thankfully Aeryon created a new story through seeking support with family and friends, a structure of nutrition, fitness and recreating thinking and behaviour patterns. Her story offers hope to others and practical strategies that support change and a new healthy way of living.

Connect with Aeryon Ashlie on her website at https://aeryonashlie.com